BELBA'S SHADOW

STORY BY: LESTER "L2" SHAW

This Book is dedicated to Bellaire Dior Shaw, Daddy loves you so much!
Always walk with confidence and your head held high,
you are the greatest!!!
Daddy loves you!!!

Belba is a shy and pretty little pig.

Having her shadow by her makes her more confident and braver.

This morning, Belba and Shadow somehow got separated by accident.

Without her shadow, Belba feels alone and nervous; her world tour is in jeopardy and her musical career is at risk!

Early one cold morning, Belba the pig bundled up before going outside. She looked fabulous!

All winter she had stayed in her cozy condo preparing for her annual performance, which now was only a day away.

Her fans were waiting to see if she and her famous shadow would emerge together.

If they did, it would mean Belba wouldn't be performing for another 6 weeks, and her fans wouldn't like that.

"Come, shadow." Belba said to her friend.

They did everything together,
"Sure" said Shadow "You know I got your back"

Belba opened the door.
It was a rainy day but the sun was shining.
The ground was covered with puddles.

The 2 friends got to the corner of Cheshire Bridge. Belba saw a shadow moving from side to side.

She thought it was an excited fan. It was waving its hands back and forth. What could it be?

Belba ran so fast she left Shadow. She was so scared she forgot her friend. She pulled the blinds down so no one could see her face. Shadow was left outside.

Shadow was now without Belba and she was feeling not so fearless! She looked up from the shadow that was waving only to see that it was a dog's shadow.

"Whose shadow are you?" asked the dog.
"I belong to Belba the Pig.
Yes that's right, the superstar herself!"
replied Shadow.

"But she left me here and I don't know what
to do!" cried Shadow.
"I'd like to help you, but if I do you're going
to have to find me a few bones" said the dog.
"We have a deal!" said Shadow.

Shadow felt very sad.
She leaned against the building with her new friend.

"I really want to be with Belba because I miss her," said Shadow.

Looking for Belba all day,
Shadow got tired and needed some rest.
"I guess I'll sleep here," she said to herself.

"With rest I'll be able to think a little better,
so I think I will take a nap!" Shadow sat in
the alley and fell asleep along with Kholer,
which was the name she gave her new
friend the dog.

Belba searched for her shadow the entire
time she was missing.
"Maybe she's under the bed or in the closet."
she thought.

She looked under her bed and in the closet,
but all she found was her fancy clothes and shoes.

"Maybe Shadow is lost!
She must be so scared.
I'm going to look for her right now!"

Belba spent all day looking for Shadow instead of practicing. The only thing she could think about was finding Shadow.

When it began to rain, Belba ran between the buildings to hide from the wind and rain.

It was dark and spooky down the alley.

Crunch! Crunch! Boom! Boom! Two cats were rumbling in the dumpster.

Shadow stepped out of the side of the dumpster.

She looked around and saw her dear friend Belba!

Belba looked down and thought she saw something move.

"Probably just another cat," she thought.

"Oh noooooo! You're not my shadow! You're a stranger! Stranger danger! Stranger danger!" shouted Belba! Belba ran out of the alley and into the street. She noticed it had stopped raining.

Shadow followed her friend into
the moonlight full of joy and gladness!
Belba wouldn't leave her behind this time!
Belba turned around at least eight times
very surprised.

"You really are my Shadow!" she said
with a huge smile.
"My Shadow! At last I've found you,
and it looks like a new friend too!"
They were the happiest they had ever been.

They practiced for the show all through the night and the next day to make up the time they had missed. The next day was the performance and the fans would be waiting!

They made their way from the tub to the bed
to get plenty of rest for the big show the next day!
Belba lay in the bed thinking,
"If the fans see us together, they will be sad.
This means I didn't learn my lesson.
I can't have stage fright any longer!

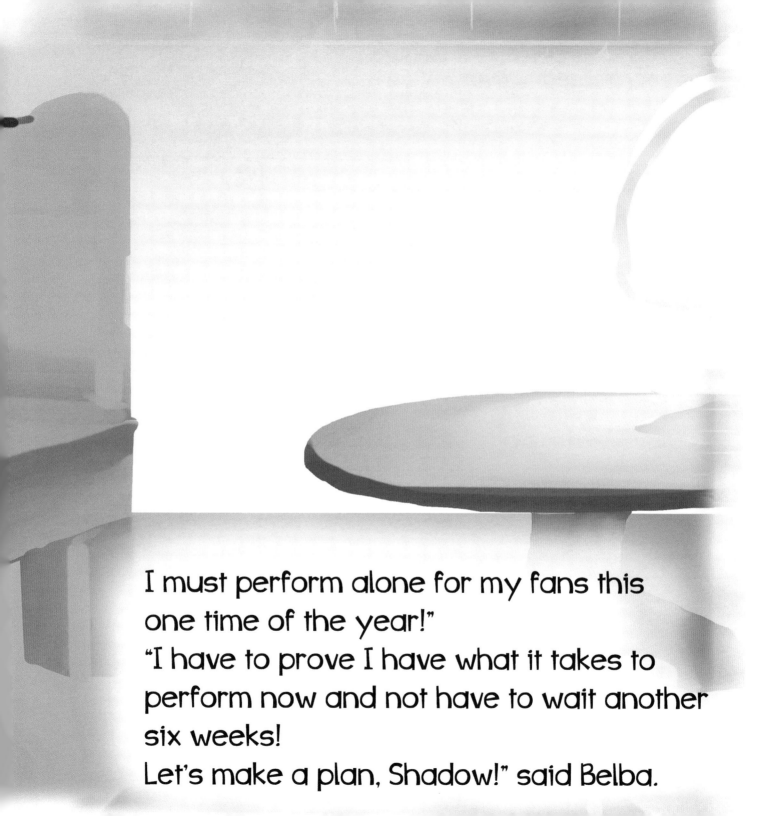

I must perform alone for my fans this one time of the year!"

"I have to prove I have what it takes to perform now and not have to wait another six weeks!

Let's make a plan, Shadow!" said Belba.

Later on that next day all of Belba's fans waited patiently on Belba to take the stage! They watched from all over the world!

"Here she comes now!" yelled one of her fans!

Belba peeked out past the stage.
When she saw her fans she had a great idea!
"Stand as close to me as you can," she whispered
to Shadow. Shadow understood!
She squeeeeeeezed in as close as she could
to her friend.

"Belba! Belba! Belba!" the fans shouted!
Belba performed on stage without her shadow!
Her fans cheered.
"WE GET TO SEE BELBA ON HER SPRING WORLD TOUR!!!"
"HER FEAR IS OVER!!!"

"Being brave finally paid off not only am I performing on my own Spring World Tour, I'm not doing it alone.

I had to overcome my fears to prove I was able to handle this tour!"
Thanks Shadow for helping me over come my fears and being a great friend to me.
We will forever be!"

Every February Belba starts her tour on the same day thanks to her best friend Shadow.
They made a pinky promise on that day that they would never split again!